*T*hink *E*xcellence . . .

*A practical, real life approach
to retail sales
"Multi Unit" store management*

*   *   *

*"Ten short chapters that will redefine how you
look at your business and lead your team."*

Library of Congress Control Number: 2010909897
ISBN: Hardcover   978-1-4535-3346-8
                Softcover   978-1-4535-3345-1
                Ebook   978-1-4535-3347-5

To order additional copies of this book, contact:
Xlibris Corporation
1-888-795-4274
www.Xlibris.com
Orders@Xlibris.com
83694

Dedicated to my wife of 20 years . . .

Whose courageous battle to fight and battle breast cancer has inspired me to fulfill my dreams.

*A practical, real life approach to retail sales
"Multi Unit" store management*

*"Ten short chapters that will redefine how you
look at your business and lead your team."*

Introduction

T hroughout my nearly three decades in retail I have witnessed many events and have worked for many individuals that displayed quite a few differing leadership styles . . . some good, some not so good. Like many of you, my retail career began at a very young age, 18 in fact, while attending college. I would often find myself thinking . . ."What would my "real" job be?" Do I REALLY enjoy what I am majoring in? Well, after receiving my Bachelor's Degree I decided to pursue a career in retail. Quite frankly I was lured by the large commission and bonus checks retail careers had the potential of producing.

As the years progressed (29 in all) and as my span of control grew from Sales Associate to Store Manager to District Manager to Region Manager to Vice President to eventually President of Sales and Operations in my current Company, I have formulated many philosophies and strategies that I believe can help young executives further their careers without enduring some of the pain I had to endure throughout my career. In retail sales management, whether you are in charge of one store or many stores, pain can come in many forms. Pain can be derived from tremendous mental stress to eventually financial burdens. Whatever form of pain a young or even seasoned veteran in business endures, much of it is "self inflicted" because of, for lack of a better word, ignorance. We either "don't know" what we "don't know" or we're embarrassed to ask questions for fear of being labeled a "weak or incompetent leader". Remember this, as a leader in business, fear of asking questions **IS INCOMPETENCE**.

I hope the following ten chapters supported by **"Twenty Think Excellences Tips"** will help you throughout your career and place things into proper perspective. This is my first attempt at authoring a book, so I must admit, I'm venturing into uncharted waters. In fact, I'm quite aware that many of my fellow executives may have differing opinions, thoughts and concepts. The reality is, that's alright. A successful executive must have confidence, but must also be open to constructive criticism. This is NO business for the "thin skinned". What I will share with you are tried and true strategies, thoughts and philosophies that have served me quite well and have proven to be very effective throughout my career. My only regret is that it took me almost three decades to accumulate this knowledge, but it feels good sharing my retail sales strategies with you today. In reality, if more executives shared their strategies openly and conversed about "best practices", their successes and subsequent failures . . . our world economy would probably be in significantly better shape today thus creating more wealth and financial stability for all.

Well . . . here we go. Please go easy on my grammar . . . enjoy . . .

Chapter One—

"Results . . . It's all about the People"

T aking short cuts to get results in the retailing business almost always ends in disaster. Unfortunately, it's a very popular technique. That short term "positive blip" on the sales report is almost always followed by some sort of "loss" that is typically greater than the short term gain. Whether it's a sales loss resulting in reduced gross profit that eventually impacts the bottom line after expenses or whether its loss prevention related, taking "people related short cuts" to drive the business is just plain "bad business". Often the results over a period of time are less than when you started. Unfortunately **impatience** drives us to look for "band aids" instead of solid candidates with the proper "skill sets" and desire to actually do the job. We want those results so badly that we are "blinded" to what is going on around us. This is a very "short sighted" approach.

Think Excellence   Tip # 1

"The reality is...results are all about the PEOPLE".

Is it always product and price?

In retailing you'll always hear about product and price. I wish I had this "widget" to sell or I wish I had the ability to charge "that price". Now, let's not be naïve, product and price are important. However, they are typically NOT the defining factor in your success as a "multi unit manager" in the retailing profession. In fact, as the economy tightens up consumers very often are looking for a **fair price**, but **demand** quality service as well. This is why you typically see companies change their advertising and marketing approach during difficult economic times. They talk more about their PEOPLE and how they "value the consumer" and less about the product. If you really want to be successful over the long haul, care about your customers ALL THE TIME. **This starts with caring about the people that work for you who actually service "that customer".**

Are you a "Super Store Manager"?

As management one must ask the question, "Who is representing my business"? Remember, as a "multi unit" retail manager you are not able to be with every manager or associate 100% of the time. It's impossible. This is precisely why the step from single store management to "multi unit" store management is such a BIG step in one's managerial career. A step that some can never make because they do not possess the proper "skill sets". They may lack delegation, follow-up or communication skills. If you want to be successful at the "multi unit" managerial level, you must refrain from hiring individuals "out of necessity" and with impatience. If you do this, you will never achieve the level of consistent profitable growth, professional success or personal satisfaction you are looking for. **Your success will be based on "luck of the draw" rather**

than on calculated decisions and good "old fashioned" common sense. If you cringe when you ask yourself, "Who is representing my business", you probably have a problem that is in need of correction. If you avoid the problem, you'll find yourself being a **"super store manager"** . . . TRYING to do everything on your own. The end result will probably be the ultimate failure of your business and YOUR eventual demotion or even dismissal from the company, a company which you may love, **despite your hard work and efforts**.

I typically refrain from using sports analogies because some folks are simply not sports fans. I happen to be a huge sport fan. However, there is one sports analogy that I believe many of us can relate to. If you think of a quarterback on a football team, his job is to distribute the football to either a running back, tight end or wide receiver with the end result being the advancement of the football across the goal line . . . scoring points. A "multi unit" store manager MUST do the same thing. They must delegate tasks and assignments, distributing the ball if you like, with the ultimate outcome being the increase in sales and profits. HOW do you do this without the RIGHT PEOPLE? The minute a "multi unit" manager tries to do everything on their own inefficiency will set in resulting in lost or reduced profits.

So how do you get the right people to work for you?

Let's keep this simple, in retail sales it really boils down to three things. Finding a team with the *right* . . .

- *Personality*
- *Desire and*
- *Skill Sets*

Think Excellence   *Tip #2*

"Build a team with the **RIGHT** personality, desire and skill sets for the positions you are attempting to fill."

First of all you must determine what type of skill sets your candidate must possess. Since this book is about retail sales, let's stick to recruiting for a retail position. Remember to **"hire based on personality and inherent skill sets, train for desired results".** This is pretty straight forward. The point . . . if you are hiring for a retail sales related position, why would you recruit someone that doesn't smile? Someone that doesn't enjoy being around people? You see too many folks look at retailing as just something to do "in between" **real jobs**. The problem is that management hires these individuals and eventually promotes them "out of necessity" to manage their stores! Then they wonder why their business is failing. It's comical. It's also very sad. Consumers deserve better. In any retailing business one could look at an individual store within a market that has been performing below standards for quite some time. Finally a management change is made. Eureka! Suddenly the sales and performance of the location "skyrocket". Why? Was it a miracle? Or did we simply put a manager in place that possessed the appropriate skill sets . . . the right retailing personality to do the job correctly? The product was the same. The pricing was the same. The advertising strategy was the same. **The difference in the performance was directly related to THE PEOPLE.** Sure you can say you made a management change and shipped the store new merchandise or ran a "Re-Grand Opening Event" or perhaps did some special advertising. But when you really get down to it, the customers responded to the "personality" of the new manager . . . period.

Some recruiting tips from someone who's made plenty of mistakes . . .

Here are some "key recruiting tips" that helped me a great deal as I matured later on in my career. The reality is, in retailing, good recruiting does NOT have to be an expensive proposition. Very often the best techniques are pretty inexpensive, *if not "free"*. Now don't get me wrong. There are many advanced methods to recruit that are quite good and necessary at times. Unfortunately they can be quiet expensive. In today's economic, cost sensitive environment, is that expense really justified? "Spending money in business to better your business is NOT a bad thing. **Spending money foolishly in business is inexcusable!"**

*T*hink *E*xcellence   *T*ip #*3*

"Spending money in business to better your business is NOT a bad thing. Spending money foolishly in business is inexcusable!"

Let's take a look at some recruiting tips . . .

- *Hire based on personality and inherent skill sets, train for desired results . . .*
  - You can develop certain "selling skills" but keep in mind . . .
  - You cannot change someone's "inherit" personality . . ."If they are in sales and they do NOT like to smile . . . stay away from them!"

- *Be very clear when discussing compensation if you have a "Performance Based Pay Plan" . . .*
  - Someone NOT used to sales may be looking for a high base salary

- If your pay plan is "performance based", **recruit "self motivated" individuals that are accustomed to this form of compensation**

*Competitive recruiting **with "class"** . . . it's very effective . . .*
- "Shop" your competition—Do the employees look happy?
- If they look frustrated . . . **tactfully** ask them if they may be looking for a change
    - Note: Don't embarrass their current manager, that is unprofessional and a very poor practice.
- Recruit individuals that are already in service related professions
    - Fast food companies
    - Restaurant waiters and waitresses
    - Specialty retail stores
        - Be careful if you are recruiting from a "big box" and you are a "small box" company . . . remember "skill sets"
    - Successful entrepreneurs looking for more stability

Internet/web based recruiting—a great tool, but be careful . . .
- NEVER hire someone without physically meeting them and sitting down with them "face to face"

Customer/Client recruiting—very often your customers are very knowledgeable about the products you sell . . .
- Some of the most loyal and potentially best producing employees are **current customers**
- They also serve as great recruiters themselves . . . **think about that!**

- o Through your dealings with them **you already know a little about their personality, skill sets, etc.**

🔸 *Vary your "recruiting practices" . . .*
  - o "Mix it up" a bit . . .
    - Don't deprive yourself of finding some talent because you are set in your recruiting ways!
    - Practice different recruiting methods, perfecting your technique and skills

🔸 *CAUTION: Don't build your business on "part timers" ONLY . . .*
  - o While part-timers are good on occasion . . . you must have maturity, stability and LOYALTY on your team as well
  - o If your "part-time mix" is far *greater* than your full time mix, you **may** have an issue, **be careful!**

There you have it, seven very valuable "tips" for effective and efficient recruiting. Try it, I'm certain you will find they work for you as well.

The 3 Categories of Employees

Very often as a "multi unit" store manager in the retailing industry you will find yourself beating your head against the wall over employee issues. Keep in mind, every second you spend doing this you are taking precious time away from training your people, developing them and subsequently enhancing your sales and profits. It seems like the more individuals you talk to about this topic for guidance, *the more confused you can get.* **So let's simplify shall we**. There really are only three types of employees. I have grouped them into three categories . . .

- *Category 1 Employees*—This group is made up of employees and managers that possess the "skill sets" and attitude to make a positive impact on your business. **They are willing to learn and embrace change as business trends demand.**

- *Category 2 Employees*—This group is made up of employees and managers that possess the "skill sets" to make a positive impact on your business, but rather they select to use their skill sets in a **"negative fashion"**. They display a negative demeanor and attitude towards your customers and Company.

- *Category 3 Employees*—This group is made up of employees and managers that possess the right attitude and are willing to learn. Unfortunately they **do not** possess the appropriate "skill sets" to be an effective employee or manager in your particular business.

Think about it. Those are the three categories most, if not ALL, employees fall into. Ask yourself periodically, **"How many Category 2 and 3 employees do I have on payroll?"** If the answer is quite a few . . . . **your business is in trouble!**

Category 3 employees really hurt from a "personal perspective". Very often they are very loyal to the company and are actually trying very hard to succeed. They simply do not possess the skill sets. The longer you keep these individuals on payroll, the longer your performance will suffer. Ultimately it will impact your personal income, as well as, the profits of the organization. If you are a good leader . . . you must be honest with them when conducting performance reviews.

Category 2 employees are just "sad". They are the very worst representation of your business and MUST be dealt with. Their negative attitude is like a disease that is devouring the morale of your personnel. Whatever the reason is . . . passed up for promotion, commission or bonus issue . . . if you cannot correct their behavior and get them BACK to a **Category 1** status, you must remove them from your team. The negative ramifications that can come from retaining **Category 2** employees on payroll is significant. For one thing, **Category 1** employees **do not want** to work with **Category 2** employees. Would you? Not to mention . . . what happens if a perspective employee enters one of your locations and is met by a **Category 2** employee? Not a great way to recruit talent. A **Category 2** employee has this thought process . . ."*I don't want anyone "good or positive" working here. That might jeopardize this crappy job that I don't want to lose!*"

The bottom line, strive to recruit and staff your team with **Category 1** employees and managers. They are not only strong producers, but they are very good recruiters as well. *The RIGHT employees that you train and develop along the way, will benefit your Company in many positive ways.*

Surround yourself with great people and you'll win . . ."Maybe!"

As a "multi unit retail manager" you'll hear plenty of times, "Just surround yourself with great people! That's all it takes! You'll always win!" Think about how many times you've heard this in seminars. **This could NOT be further from the truth.** Now, before you think I'm crazy, let me explain. The reason I say this is because you are missing a "critical piece" to the phrase. Anyone you recruit that is "worth their salt" **wants to be developed in one way or another.** Perhaps they are looking for growth within the Company . . . just like you. They may have families and wish to strive for greater earnings, commission or bonus. If you don't care about their development . . . even though they are "great as individuals" . . . they will eventually elect to leave your team. You then find yourself back at square one once again. As a result productivity and profits decline as you search for a "qualified" replacement. So the correct phrase is . . ."Surround yourself with great people **and genuinely care about their professional development** and you will win!"

Chapter Two—

The 3 C's to **Efficient** and **Effective** leadership

Being a leader of a "multi unit" retailing business is tough enough. What you don't want to do is work against yourself. Inadvertently the boss can, at times, be the greatest negative influence within a business. It's not done intentionally, but it happens. Stress comes from ALL sides and angles. It comes from your superiors "above you", it comes from customers, it comes from your team members that report to you, it comes from vendors, it comes from your family and it can comes from your peers. *That's a bit overwhelming for anyone.*

With that said you must remember the "3C's to efficient and effective leadership". They are . . .

- *Remain "Calm" . . . communicate clearly!*
- *Remain "Confident" . . . Do Not doubt your abilities . . . but don't be foolish!*
- *Remain "Connected" with your Team . . . DO NOT alienate them!*

Remain "Calm"

As the leader you are going to face adversity. How you deal with the adversity will define you as a leader. Keep this next statement in mind and memorize it . . ."The difference between 'Failure and Success' lies very often in one's ability to lead their team through obstacles while doing the little things . . . <u>RIGHT</u>. The smallest activities can grow into the largest successes, eventually defining the character of your team & the legacy of your leadership."

When you lose your "cool" your people will sense it. They will all react in many different ways. Some will lash out negatively, some will shut down and become useless, some will simply leave. I'm not saying you must be a "zombie", this will surely put your team to sleep. What I am saying is that you can me motivational and uplifting throughout difficult times, displaying energy and passion, yet still remain "calm" and in control. Losing your cool will almost certainly lead to poor decisions and subsequent re-evaluation of previous direction. This creates additional frustration and tension within your team and it is **inefficient and quite ineffective.**

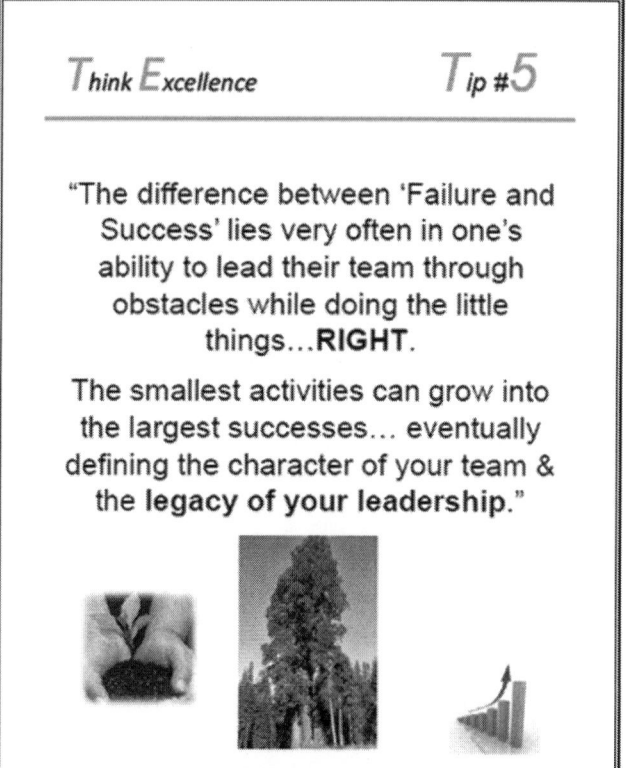

*T*hink *E*xcellence   *T*ip #5

"The difference between 'Failure and Success' lies very often in one's ability to lead their team through obstacles while doing the little things...**RIGHT**.

The smallest activities can grow into the largest successes... eventually defining the character of your team & the **legacy of your leadership**."

Remain Confident

Confidence in any leadership position is essential for success. In the retailing business if you are in charge of "multi units" it takes on an even higher level of significance. Your team will "respond positively" to you if they are confident of your leadership skills. Understand what I just said, they will **RESPOND POSTIVELY** to you. There is a big difference between individuals simply "working for you" versus "responding positively" to your leadership style. Remember, your decisions will most likely impact, whether positively or negatively, their income through increased or decreased commission and bonus payouts. If you do NOT appear "confident" to your team, they will hesitate when following through on direction or initiatives. They will "sense" your lack of confidence and it will come back to haunt you. Very often this will lead to the failure of a project **that SHOULD have succeeded.** Why did it fail? Think about it. It failed because you did not get the support of your team. Could it have been because you communicated the plan in a very "tentative" fashion **without confidence**? You bet!

Now, don't be foolish. If, through the collection of new or additional facts, you realize you have provided the wrong direction to your team . . . **CHANGE DIRECTION IMMEDIATELY.** Don't be foolish and keep proceeding down the wrong path that you now **KNOW** is wrong. "Check your ego at the door" and change direction. Be honest with your team and more often than not, they will respect this. The next time, try to have all the facts BEFORE you direct your team. **In the real world . . . this is NOT always possible.**

Remain Connected

As a "multi unit" retail manager your greatest asset is your people. Are you connected with them on a professional level? Do they feel comfortable approaching you? Do you have a "holier than thou" attitude that is intimidating, so they stay away? Do they believe you are listening to them? Do they feel as if you genuinely care about them? Do they feel that their opinion counts? Folks, these are just a few questions you must ask yourself BEFORE you answer, with confidence, that you are "connected to your people". Think of yourself as the plug on the power cord of a lamp. When the lamp is plugged in the bulb shines brightly. When the lamp is unplugged, no matter what you try to do, that bulb won't light. It's the same thing as "multi unit" retailing manager. If you are "unplugged" and not "privy" to what's going on within your business, you are opening yourself up to not just failure, **but career self destruction**. People related issues can destroy your career. You must listen to your people so you truly understand their needs and wants. Once you understand their needs and wants it's up to YOU to show them the way. Once again . . . let's not be naïve. You are the boss. There will be times when you totally disagree with your team. That's okay. Take the time to explain to them WHY you disagree. "If you take the time to explain to your team WHY something needs to be done a certain way . . . **you'll be surprised how many will comply!**"

Memorize this next statement my friends . . ."**The greatest disrespect you can give to your team is to ask them to do something without attaching the WHY! Always explain WHY!**"

*T*hink *E*xcellence   *T*ip #6

"The greatest disrespect you can give to your team is to ask them to do something without attaching the **WHY!**

Always explain **WHY!**"

Chapter Three—

Focus on what you CAN control

Getting "sidetracked" as a "multi unit" retail store manager is common. It's also potentially very dangerous. Okay, what do I mean by this? Well, there is only so much you can do in one day. Time is very precious in retailing and a leader must generate "positively results" from each activity. I refer to this as **"Rate of Return on Time Invested"** . . . RROTI for short. If you waste your time focusing your attention, worries and conversation on areas of the business which you have "zero" control over, you will find yourself chasing your competition forever. In fact, they will soon be far ahead of you and out of sight. "Focus your attention on things you can control at the store, district, region and even companywide level depending on your leadership level within an organization".

Think Excellence — Tip # 7

"Focus on what you **can control** at the store level....don't waste a second of your time worrying about what you cannot control."

Focus your attention on the . . .

- Professional development of your people,
- Efficient recruiting practices,
- Effective staffing of your stores,
- Accurate forecasting of sales,
- "In stock" position on product,
- Product "move rates",
- Sales floor "customer readiness",
- Merchandising and store display,
- Etc, etc, etc . . .

Don't worry about . . .

- Construction in a parking lot (unless you can get a rent reduction!),
- The neighboring business that is struggling,
- A product that may be on an allocation hold,
- A particular fixture that you cannot ascertain,
- A price you cannot match.

As you read this chapter think about all the time you have wasted throughout your professional career focusing your attention on things which you had "zero" control over. If you added all those hours up and multiplied them by your average hourly earnings, what would the total dollar amount of "wasted expense" be? Obviously, it's impossible to truly quantify . . . but a true executive understands this statement. Ask yourself, "Would the time have been better spent investing in the **development of your people**?" How about spending the time studying traffic patterns so that you could better schedule your personnel allowing them more "time to sell" and spend with each customer? How about spending this time "building vendor relations" or analyzing a "reinvestment of profits" back into the business? Ahhhh . . . the list goes on and on.

Rate of Return on Time Invested—RROTI

In today's economic climate a "multi unit" retail manager MUST think in terms of **"rate of return on time invested"**. As an example . . . if you spent an inordinate amount of time on a "Category 3" employee (see page 9) rather than coming to the realization that this employee just doesn't have the RIGHT "skill sets" for the job, wouldn't the **"rate of return on time invested"** be greater working with a Category 1 employee? Couldn't you generate greater "future profits" at a **faster rate** by developing the skills of the Category 1 employee? This may sound insincere, but it is the "nature of the game". Ask yourself . . . **are you playing to win?** I think you understand where I'm going with this.

Overcoming the Self Defeatist

One of the greatest battles you must face as a "multi unit" store manager is overcoming the attitude of the "self defeatist". This is the employee that constantly looks at every obstacle as "insurmountable". The reality is their attitude negatively impacts others. This employee may, in fact, be very talented . . . they may even be a solid producer. But one must ask the question . . ."**How good _could_ they be?**" At times they *become* a "Category 2" type of employee (see page 9). Your mission . . . make them a "Category 1" again! This is easier said than done.

The problem is . . .
. . . the "self defeatist" is assuming they are doing **everything possible** to WIN. Therefore the first "external obstacle" that is presented becomes

"Armageddon". The best way to handle this type of employee is to focus their attention on areas that have **"room for improvement"** within their control. With that said, you must be persistent. Their defeatist attitude can rub off on you as you are only human. Take some time to observe the employees at this particular location. Is each "individual sale" perfect? Is there room for improvement? How's the scheduling? How's the staffing? How's the product mix? The list of "controllables" goes on and on . . . .

Think Excellence   _T_ip #8

"Never assume you are doing everything **perfect**!
There is **ALWAYS** one more thing you can do to win...by the book!"

One more thing...

Chapter Four—

"Motivate with Substance" . . .

I 'm certain that at one time or another in your career you have sat through a motivational sales presentation. In fact, if you are in the sales profession, I'm certain you probably have sat through more than one. The reality is . . . some are actually very good. They are uplifting . . . they make you "feel good". The speaker very often captivates the audience. Now, following the presentation ask yourself, **"What did I actually get from the presentation that will help me manage my business?"** Sometimes the answer is . . ."not very much". Here's my point. Whenever you deliver a message to your team, whether that message is operational in nature or sales related, **deliver it with "passion"** . . . from your heart. However, also **deliver it with "substance"**. I call this . . ."**motivating with substance**". Simply motivating your team and then letting them run "on their own" will almost always net "subpar" results. As a young executive this is very often a common mistake that is made. Sure, they seem "pumped" when they leave the room . . . or log off of the conference call . . . but do they really know what to do, or more importantly **HOW** to deliver the expected results.

Think Excellence   *Tip #9*

"If you consistently give your team the proper direction you will be amazed at just how many things they will do....GREAT!"

I truly believe that motivating is an essential "skill set" of a leader. However, there are all different ways to motivate. Some deliver a "high energy" message. Some deliver a message that is more "heartfelt" and low key. One must know their audience and tailor their presentation accordingly. Whatever your style of delivery, **make certain there is a "relevant message" delivered.** The greatest disrespect one person can give another, especially as a supervisor, is to ask a subordinate to do something **without attaching the "why" to the request.** While you are delivering your motivational message, **include the activities** that must be accomplished to complete the extraordinary task or deliver the superior performance figures. The "substance" of your presentation, coupled with the proper delivery, will dictate the ultimate retention of the RIGHT message. Very often a sales team will want to satisfy "the boss" so badly they will run as fast as they can. But if they are running in the wrong direction . . . **what good is it**?

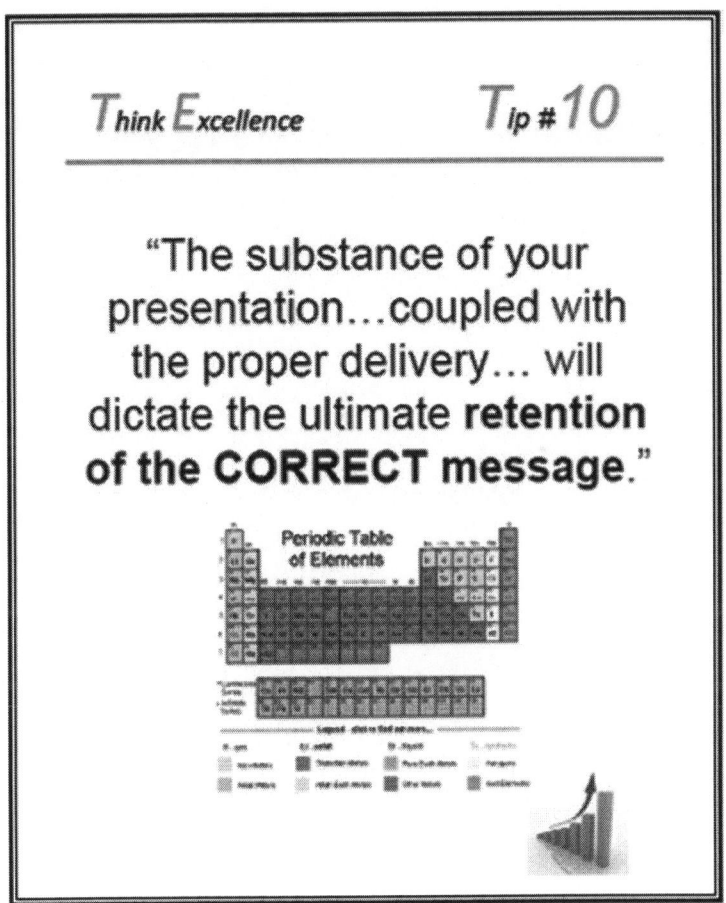

Ah responsibility. It's a big part of our job as the leader of "multi unit" retail stores. Let's not forget that you are NOT in charge of a group of machines. As the leader of a group **of individuals** one must remember that simply rallying your team may inadvertently drive the wrong or even unethical behavior. Unfortunately the wrong behavior can lead to the dismissal of an otherwise solid associate. Proper direction is essential.

*T*hink *E*xcellence   *T*ip # *11*

"Motivate with Substance"

-Simply rallying your team but not providing direction or activities is **"empty motivation"**.

This strategy may deliver a "short term burst" in performance. However, this strategy very rarely delivers **"long term positive performance"**.

Remember, your goal as a "multi unit" retail store manager is to achieve consistent profitable sales growth! Accomplish this by **motivating with substance"**.

Chapter Five—

"Define your differentiators . . ."

W hat is a "differentiator" in business? The easy answer is "anything that makes you different from the rest." Right? Well . . . actually "differentiators" in business can be very tricky. They could help you, they could hurt you. In order for your group of stores to be successful, in any competitive environment, you must first think long and hard about **what you want your "differentiators" to be.** Think of it this way, in business your "differentiators" are your *signature.* What makes your district, region, division or company different? Why should someone shop your stores and NOT the competition? Think **beyond the obvious** like, "best price in town" or "best selection". BORING! These proclamations are far too common in business today. **Your "differentiators" must be fairly unique and NOT easily replicated by the competition.** Key words here . . ."**not easily replicated**". Whatever those unique "differentiators" are, shout them out and be proud of them. It serves you no good if your team is NOT aware of what makes them special. Is it a **special "skill set"** you have recruited for? Is it a special **"service"** your team has been trained to deliver **with perfection**? Is it a special way you would like your customers handled? Etc, etc., etc . . .

Once you have decided what you want your "differentiators" to be . . . **mold your TEAM around them.** Recruit, hire, train and develop your team with these "differentiators" in mind at all times. Shy away from anything if it contradicts what you are shouting out as your "differentiator". Highlight the "differentiators" in presentations, trainings and district (Company) communications. Bring your "differentiators" to life and make them **"MORE THAN WORDS"**. When you visit your locations and conduct trainings ask yourself, "Are the 'differentiators' being exhibited by the sales team." If not, then you probably need to go back and "rethink" HOW you are communicating to your team. Don't be naïve as sometimes you need to take a close look at the actual "differentiators". **Are they STILL relevant? Are they outdated? Should they be changed?**

Finally . . . don't underestimate the importance of "differentiators". In today's business world these characteristics can make or break your business. Like I mentioned earlier, "WHY should a customer shop in one of your locations versus the competition?" Remember, we stated earlier that "results are all about the people". Make certain your people possess the skill sets to deliver on your promised "differentiators". Little things, **done RIGHT,** make the greatest difference in business. (See tip #5)

Think Excellence   *Tip #12*

What are your **"differentiators"**?

You must determine what you want your team to be famous for. These will become your "differentiators".

Your team signature!

Chapter Six—

"Define your path to success" . . .

A s you review the previous five chapters it's clear that we've addressed quite a bit already. As a new or even veteran "multi unit" store manager you must take some quite, quality time to define not only your personal path to success, **but that of your business as well**. What direction do you want your team to take in order to deliver the desired results? This must be clearly dictated. A "path to success" needs to outline certain specific "sets of criteria" that must be followed by all. Each "set of criteria" is made up of "guidelines". Discipline in business is essential, but with understanding typically comes compliance. It's important to keep in mind that you do NOT want "puppets" working for you. Everyone will have their own "selling style". As long as their style supports your "differentiators" and delivers desired results within your outlined guidelines, that's okay.

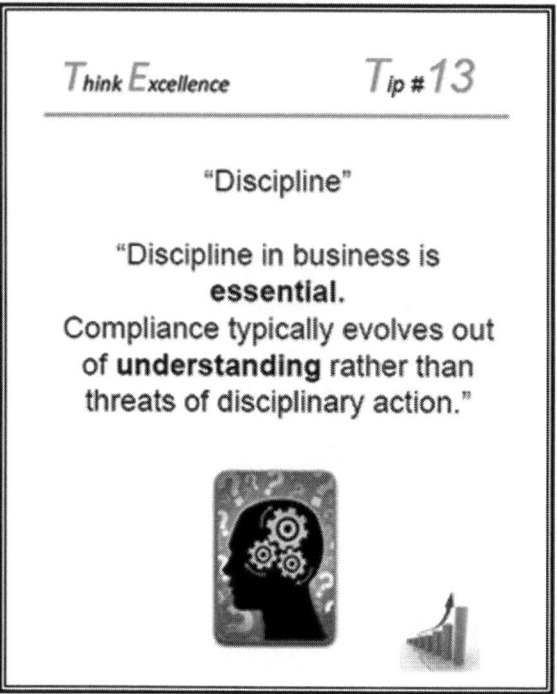

Think Excellence   *Tip #13*

"Discipline"

"Discipline in business is **essential.**
Compliance typically evolves out of **understanding** rather than threats of disciplinary action."

As an executive in charge of multiple locations the morale of your team is very important. Make certain your "path to success" is tied into increased earnings for your sales team not simply your personal gain. Very often, not always, this will enhance morale. Here's my point . . . if you have defined a "path to success" which will increase the profitability of your market . . . and it does not enhance the earnings of your team . . . **you will NEVER gain their full support.** Make certain your team can translate "the path" into increased earnings for themselves, as well as, the ability to deliver a better quality of life for their families. Following the "path to success" should ensure that all "key" activities, **fundamental profit driving activities,** are rewarded. Once you get the support of your team . . . because they have experienced financial reward while following "the path" . . . **the majority typically follow along**.

Clear explanation of each step is critical as well. Explain each step along the way and explain "why" it so important. Tie the "step" into enhanced earnings and personal satisfaction. Bring each step to life and use "real life" examples to make your point. Don't be afraid to share your personal business experiences within boundaries. This will enhance your "street credibility" in the eyes of your sales team and direct reports. In "multi unit" retail store management there is no degree that is worth more than experience and credibility. Remember "Tip #10" on page 19 . . . always explain **"WHY"**!

Belief" drives results . . . both positive and negative! If you ask your team to do something they "believe in" which, in turn, will drive positive results . . . most will comply! Conversely, if you ask your team to do something they "believe in" that will drive negative results, most will comply as well. **This can be very dangerous!**

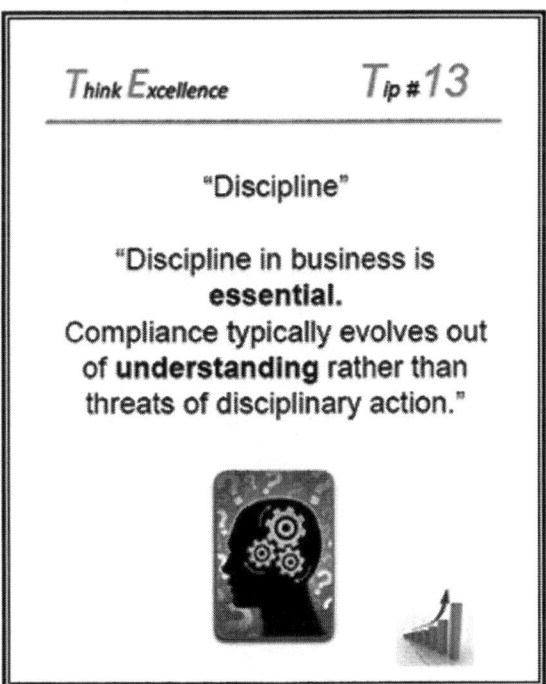

Think Excellence   Tip #13

"Discipline"

"Discipline in business is **essential.**
Compliance typically evolves out of **understanding** rather than threats of disciplinary action."

Chapter Seven—

"House of Cards" vs. "Castle" management

I n business you'll typically notice two types of dominant management styles exhibited by leaders. I call these two styles "house of cards" management and "castle" management styles. Allow me to explain. "House of Cards" management is a style that typically pays off with short term, often short lived gains. It's a style in sales that generates inconsistent pay because your results are not sustainable because it lacks true substance, continuity, structure and very little development of the team around you. Therefore you may have one month or quarter that delivers fantastic results followed by three or four quarters that deliver poor results. In the end, when you tally your earnings from bonus and commissions, you probably did not earn a great deal of money. However, due to that one month or quarter of success you **THINK you had**, you then tend to live well "over your head" and find yourself in considerable debt when the dust settles and you realize you really weren't that good after all.

To add to the problems associated with this management style, "House of Cards" management typically does not allow the executive in charge to have any "quality of life" because you are constantly "shooting from the hip". Without a predetermined, well thought out plan your strategy is constantly changing. This leads to poor decision making and uncontrolled "stress levels". High stress levels from business, as well as, high stress levels from family are a sure fire recipe for disaster. It also leads to high turnover within your team because quality individuals typically do not like working within this environment for elongated periods of time. Any executive "worth their salt" craves development. If not received, they will move on.

Finally, the "House of Cards" management style lends itself to a false "sense of security". You may think you are doing well. You may "think" your team is performing. However, quite rebellion "behind the scenes" can lead to a very quick collapse resulting in very poor results. This style has no real substance or infrastructure. For this reason I call it the "House of Cards" management style.

Conversely, let's look at the "Castle" management style. The "Castle" management style delivers long term gains. In essence it is a style that delivers consistent "personal and professional" growth. It is a style that is built to withstand changes in the business, adjustments to strategy and unexpected turnover. This management style is built around the development of the people within your organization thus establishing a solid, loyal foundation. The benefits of this management style are plentiful. To name a few . . .

- Consistent "personal and professional" growth
- More than adequate income
  - Enabling you to plan for your future "needs and wants"
- Fruitful "quality of life"
- Controlled "stress levels"
- SUBSTANTIATED "sense of security"
  - Proven over TIME

The "success key" to this management style is strong recruiting and low turnover stemming from the use of "proven" recruiting and people management strategies. The low turnover rate lends itself to a more experienced team. An experienced and motivated team with a high degree of self worth typically performs at a higher level with consistency . . . consistency being the "key word".

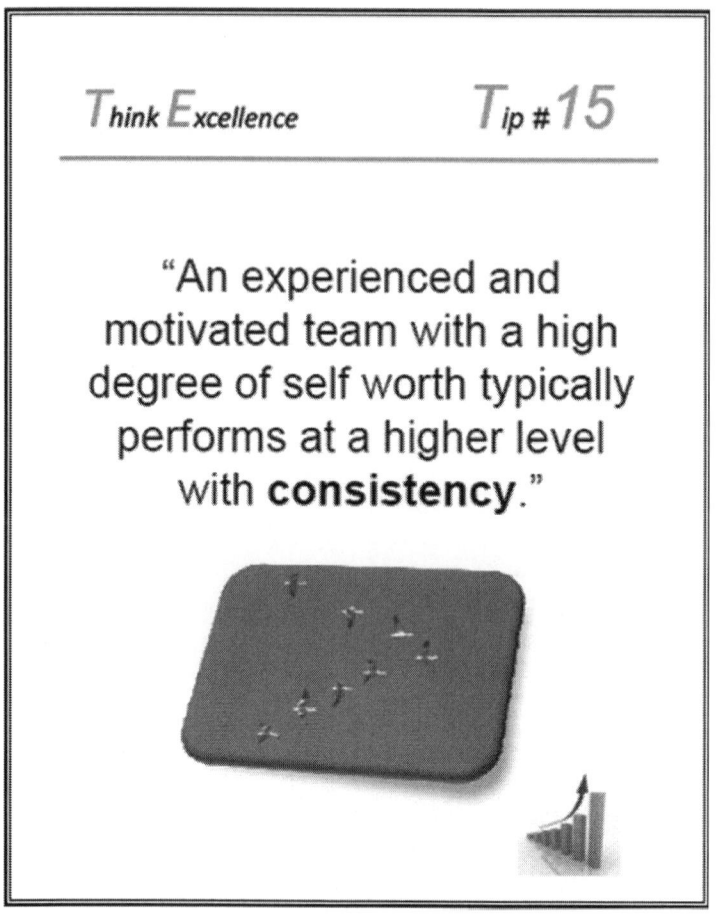

*T*hink *E*xcellence   *T*ip # *15*

"An experienced and motivated team with a high degree of self worth typically performs at a higher level with **consistency**."

Chapter Eight—

"Don't go to Vegas and sit at the Blackjack table if you can't count to 21!"

As a "multi unit retail store manager" there is one thing for certain, many team members do NOT understand their pay plan. Think about the negative ramifications of this. If a pay plan is designed properly its intent is to enhance various "key metrics" within the business. These metrics should not only stimulate sales, but they should foster profitable growth as well. Obviously you want your sales team to be compensated by driving metrics that enhance Company profits. So if you put all your energy into developing a pay plan that touches all "key metrics" within your business but the team which is getting paid to deliver results DOES NOT understand this . . . **what good is it?**

I ask you . . .

"Would you go to Vegas and sit at the Blackjack table if you couldn't count to 21?"

Of course not . . . although at times it does seem as if some folks sure do! If your team understands their pay plan, **and that pay plan is designed properly,** your profits will increase dramatically as they strive to increase their earnings. Subsequently tie all your initiatives into your team's pay plan. Explain how . . .

- If they do "this" . . . they will enhance their bonus or commission by "this much".
  - **Bring their pay plan to life.**

The more you discuss their pay plan and tie it into activities surrounding sales and profit performance, the more they will make the "realistic" correlation between performance and pay. In a perfect world, great performance should always generate great compensation. The question is . . ."**What is the definition of GREAT performance?**"

*T*hink *E*xcellence   *T*ip # *16*

"A pay plan must **NOT** be looked at as a component of cost...but rather as a source of profit generation."

Very often we talk about various tasks that need to be accomplished . . . however we neglect to tie it back to their pay structure. **What a waste!** A pay plan must become more than simply words on a piece of paper. It must "resonate" with success, better quality of life, better schools for the children, etc. Do NOT underestimate the POWER that the "Human Factor" can bring to your business. Yes, money is NOT the only motivator. But one's inability to "pay the family bills" is one of the biggest "demotivators" I know!

Design your pay plan or incentives to maximize a specific metric within the profit equation. Keep in mind, in its simplest form . . . **Profit = (Sales X GM%) - Cost**. It doesn't matter what business you are in. If your "cost" is greater than your "Gross Profit" . . . you are **BANCRUPT!** If you are looking to maximize sales . . . watch your GM line **very closely**.

- Will the GP $'s generated offset the cost associated to the incentive/promotion?
- What about the cost?
  - Will the incentive drive up cost at a disproportional dollar amount compared to GP? If so . . . why would you do it?
  - **Are you selling yourself "out of business"?**

These are basic questions that are so often overlooked or neglected. They are neglected because of inefficiency or a poorly designed pay plans. If someone is getting rich driving sales at the expense of profit . . . **you have a huge "hole in your boat"**. FIX IT . . . before it is too late.

Think Excellence   *Tip #17*

Build your sales culture around the concept of **"profitable growth"** and always ask yourself…

"Will my pay plan enhance profits?
Does it **DRIVE** the **RIGHT** behavior?"

Chapter Nine—

"You don't have customers . . . you have GUESTS!"

Think about this next question, "Do you have customers or do you have guests?" Whatever it is you are selling . . . someone comes into your place of business to purchase something . . . anything. The reality is they are "guests" in a location you simply rent. They may or may not purchase anything at your location. Does that mean they should get treated differently from those that actually purchase something? Obviously the answer is **"no"**. We **must** treat our customers as if they are guests in our home. I know this might sound odd . . . but think about what I am saying for a moment. Don't you want your guests to be **comfortable** in your home? You want them to feel **relaxed** and **welcome**. Wouldn't you want your "customers" to feel the same way? The reality is, when a person walks into your business they are initially a "guest". Hopefully that "guest" is transformed into a "guest" that decides to make a purchase as well.

Observe a business owner who greets every "guest" personally as they enter his/her place of business. This owner "gets it". He or she has added the personal touch to their business. Remember, **professional relationships are built between PEOPLE . . . NOT companies.** Once a "guest" is relaxed and comfortable within your place of business, the entire selling process changes. It develops into a conversation between friends. The reality is the "guest" most likely requires a product you sell . . . feeling welcome in a place of business stimulates sales that may not be made in less inviting locations.

The sad reality in today's business world is that in many cases the customers are simply taken for granted. Their money is NOT appreciated

Think Excellence

by those that desire their business. Whenever the economy is taking an "upswing" . . . the consumer is **neglected**. Businesses will never admit this . . . but, in many cases, it's true. Conversely, when the economy takes a downturn all the advertising and "in store" signage turns to "customer appreciation" with promises of **endless satisfaction** based on their decision to purchase a product. **The appreciation of a "Guest" needs to supersede business trends or "states of the economy".** Without the "guests" patronizing your stores . . . your entire team, including yourself, simply do not have a job . . . period. Therefore the most precious commodity we have as business leaders or "multi unit" store managers are our Guests.

Ask yourself . . .

- Is your place of business inviting?
- Is it too "sterile"?
- Does your store environment create a sense of "relaxation" for the Guest?
- Are your sales associates friendly?
- Are your sales associates intimidating?
- Does your sales team invite questions?
- Does your sales team TRULY care about your guests "needs and wants"?

These are just a few questions you need to answer. If any of the questions are answered in a "negative" fashion, you have an issue, fix it. Growing a business based on the "Guest Experience" versus a "Customer Experience" are two different things. Growing a business based on the "Guest Experience" is very much like tending to and nurturing a garden. If you feed a garden or water a garden too much you will typically harm the vegetable or plant. However, if you nurture the plant or vegetable with just the right amount of food and water . . . in the appropriate environment . . . it will flourish and spread. The same can be said for a "guest". Treat the "guest" professionally, offering just the right amount of interaction and "space" to think, in a friendly and inviting environment and you will see your existing business and referrals grow. This may be a strange analogy, but it does make sense. Remember what I said earlier, without the "guest" we simply do NOT have a job.

Think Excellence   Tip #19

The most precious commodity we have as business leaders or "multi unit store managers" are our Guests.

Chapter Ten—

"Run your business with your head, your heart and COMMON SENSE!"

My final chapter addresses a topic that can make a resounding impact on your leadership style and thought process. We've all heard of TLC . . ."tender loving care". Well, now I'm going to tell you about "HHC". In business it's imperative that you understand the necessity to lead your team with your . . .

+ Head,
+ Heart & . . . **above all** . . .
+ Common Sense

That's right . . ."HHC". As a leader you are dealing with people . . . people typically with families. Whether we like it or not, emotions get in the way of actions. A leader must accept this and understand it. A loyal team that reports to you can be a formidable strength in today's business world. From purely a bottom line perspective, **excessive turnover is expensive.** It's a cost that has many negative ramifications on any business. Maintaining a tenured team enables you to focus on "advanced development" versus "Training 101" **over and over again**.

You'll hear many executives say they make their decisions with "facts only". How true is this statement in **"REALITY"?** When making decisions, ask yourself . . .

- . . ."The tangible **facts** are telling me this . . . now depending on the situation . . .
- . . ."What does my **heart** tell me to do?"
- . . . finally, "What does **common sense** dictate?"

It's the ability to combine these three thought processes when coming to a decision that makes a STRONG leader. Each situation is unique and different if it deals with PEOPLE. Each situation has its own unique nuances and ramifications. Don't just "jump to a conclusion" because you reviewed facts on a piece of paper. First of all . . . who collected the facts? Could they have a bias one way or another whether knowingly or unknowingly? Again, street smarts and common sense need to bring this possibility to mind. Of course there is a time when facts will outweigh your heart. That's just business. There are times when your heart MUST outweigh "the facts". **However, there is NEVER a time when "common sense" should be outweighed by the facts or the heart.** Finding leaders with common sense in business is not an easy task. It's too easy to make that "quick decision" and move onto the next problem without **REALLY** thinking about the long term ramifications of your actions or decision. When you find a leader that is not afraid to exercise a "non popular" decision based on good 'ole common sense . . . you've got yourself a "winner". When interviewing or considering that individual to work alongside you or manage one of your locations don't get caught up with ONLY the Grade Point Average or fancy resume. Ask situational "what if" questions and see how they react without time to prepare an answer. If they provide you with an answer, whether you agree or disagree, that was derived from "common sense" . . . you probably have yourself a future leader that can be developed.

Now, ask yourself . . . do you make decisions with your head, heart and common sense on a consistent basis? Do you practice "HHC" decision making? As the leader of "multi unit" retail locations . . . **you must lead by example**. Exercising poor thought process and making decisions without touching on the "human aspect" of the job is a mistake. It's actually part of the "House of Cards" management style we spoke of in chapter 7. Remember, short term success built on a weak foundation almost always leads to long term failure and loss of profits.

Think Excellence   *Tip #20*

There is **NEVER** a time when "common sense" should be outweighed by the facts or the heart.

The Final Word—

Well, that's all I have. I hope these ten short chapters "opened your eyes" and enable you to look at your business in an entirely different way as you move through your career. Remember, **results are all about the people**. You may not agree with all my thoughts, ideas and philosophies, but you must admit, they do make you "think".

We can all "over complicate" many issues in business. The reality is most problems can be traced back to **PEOPLE**. Either the wrong people recruited or the strong people NOT developed. As the leader, our decisions considerably impact both of these scenarios. Take care of your people and develop their skills. More often than not the positive results will clearly outweigh the negative. **It's the difference between a job and a "way of life".** Look at your people . . . **BEFORE** you look at the P&L. Think about it.

Think Best!

Think People!

Think Excellence!

Take care my friends . . .

*T*hink *E*xcellence *T*ips . . .

1. "The reality is . . . results are all about **the people**".

2. "Build a TEAM with the **RIGHT** personality, desire and skill sets for the positions you are attempting to fill."

3. "Spending money in business to better your business is NOT a bad thing. Spending money foolishly in business is **inexcusable!**"

4. "Surround yourself with GREAT people and **genuinely** CARE about their PROFESSIONAL DEVELOPMENT and you will win!"

5. "The difference between 'Failure and Success' lies very often in one's ability to lead their team through obstacles while doing the **little things** . . . <u>RIGHT</u>. The smallest activities can grow into the largest successes . . . eventually defining the character of your team & the legacy of your leadership."

6. "The greatest disrespect you can give to your team is to ask them to do something w<u>ithout attaching the WHY</u>! **Always explain WHY!**"

7. "Focus on what you **can control** at the store level . . . . don't waste a second of your time worrying about what you cannot control."

8. "Never assume you are doing everything perfect! There is ALWAYS one more thing you can do to win . . . **by the book!**"

9. Proper Direction—"If you consistently give your team the proper direction you will be amazed at just how many things they will do . . . . **GREAT!**"

10. "The **substance of your presentation** . . . coupled with the proper delivery . . . will dictate the ultimate retention of the RIGHT message."

11. Motivate with Substance—"Simply rallying your team but not providing direction or activities is "empty motivation". This strategy may deliver a "<u>short term burst</u>" in performance. However, this strategy very rarely delivers "<u>long term performance</u>". Remember, your goal as a "multi unit" retail store manager is to achieve **consistent profitable sales growth**! Accomplish this by motivating with substance".

12. What are your "differentiators"?—You must determine what you want your team to be famous for. These will become your "differentiators". **Your team signature!**

13. Discipline—"Discipline in business is essential. Compliance typically **evolves out of understanding** rather than using the "baseball bat" technique."

14. **"Belief" drives results** . . . both positive and negative! If you ask your team to do something they "believe in" which, in turn, will drive positive results . . . most will comply! Conversely . . . if you ask

your team to do something they "believe in" that will drive negative results . . . most will comply as well. Very dangerous!

15. "An experienced and motivated team with a high degree of self worth typically performs at a higher level **with consistency**."

16. "A pay plan must NOT be looked at as a component of cost . . . but rather as a **source of profit generation**."

17. Build your sales culture around the concept of "profitable growth" and always ask yourself . . ."Will my pay plan enhance profits? **Does it DRIVE the RIGHT behavior**?"

18. A "guests" needs to be made to feel . . .
    a. **Comfortable,**
    b. **Relaxed and**
    c. **Welcome**

19. The most precious commodity we have as business leaders or "multi unit store managers" are our **Guests**.

20. There is **NEVER** a time when "common sense" should be outweighed by the facts or the heart.

Printed in Great Britain
by Amazon.co.uk, Ltd.,
Marston Gate.